THE WHITE EFFECT
– yeh baby!

The Power Of Auditory Messages

....

ANGI EGAN

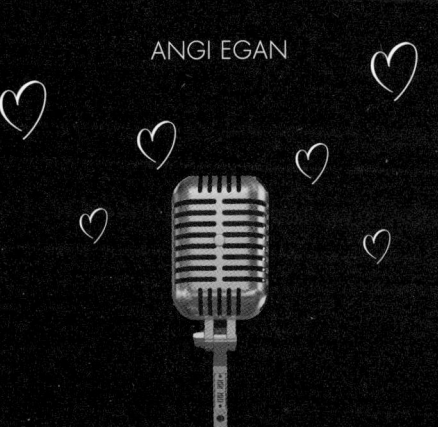

THE BARRY WHITE EFFECT
– yeh baby!

The Barry White Effect – yeh baby!
The Power Of Auditory Messages
© Angi Egan.

ISBN: 978-1-906316-56-3

All rights reserved.

Published in 2010 by Word4Word (an imprint of HotHive Books), Evesham, UK.
www.thehothive.com

The right of Angi Egan to be identified as the author of this work has been asserted by her in accordance with the Copyright, Designs and Patents Act 1988.

A CIP record of this book is available from the British Library.

No part of this publication may be reproduced in any form or by any means without permission from the author.

Printed in the UK by Latimer Trend, Plymouth.

Liz
Keep Shining
Angi B

Preface

Preface

I have been involved with sales, service and the world of commerce for almost 25 years. Running parallel to this has been my 'interesting' relationship history. These combined experiences are the inspiration behind the Romancing the Customer™ series of business guides. I draw the parallel between great romance and great business simply because there are so many wonderful comparisons to be made, it offers much amusement, and finally it is a powerful metaphor which appears to hold wide appeal. People just 'get it'.

Haven't we all, at some time in our lives, experienced the exciting thrill and all-embracing feelings of being in love – be it with someone or something? The besotted thoughts, the impulsive actions, the anticipation, the irrational, uncharacteristic behaviour … the closest most of us get to feelings of madness.

Then one day something happens to change our feelings forever – be it the insidious and steadily corrosive descent of boredom, the wonder of what else exists, or the fiery rejection of betrayal. The promise of great romance is lost. The relationship is finished. The lure of another becomes too tempting to resist.

Next, let's run the parallel with businesses and their customers.

As businesses we woo them, do whatever it takes to win their hearts, secure their loyalty, gain their trust and let them see that no other can anticipate their every need quite like we can. There is a similar thrill and exhilaration with the chase, we constantly wonder if they're going to choose us, in fact the anticipation is sometimes just too much to bear.

Then somehow we start to take them for granted. We stop making them feel special. We start making excuses. We forget. We get too busy. We allow them to become bored by our predictability, we only ever contact them when we want something, we start to believe the little things no longer matter, we start to put our needs before theirs. Inevitably they start to develop wanderlust, they compare you with another, they dally with promiscuity, they start to imagine life without you, and finally they move on.

It would be wonderful to announce I was the originator of the customer service message, that I am the first person to foster the notion of strong

PREFACE

customer relationships. Of course neither is true. The truth is that despite there being a small rainforest of books detailing the virtues of customer service and an avalanche of online information about business relationships, service in the UK still sucks.

A global recession appears to have done little to improve the situation – in many ways it has engendered an acute fondness for the 'computer says no' mentality. An attitude which offers frustrated consumers excuses, blame and justification for poor service by hiding behind company policy.

The Romancing the Customer™ business guides offer an insight into ways you may be unwittingly damaging your customer relationships and, more importantly, demonstrate the steps you can take to stop this from happening.

The Barry White Effect – yeh baby! is designed to enlighten, entertain and highlight the powerful effect our words have on those around us. Let us not be lazy with language. The English language is one of the richest in the world. Language needs to be fun, jargon-free and enriching. Let's explore how to use words to create intensity, desire, humour, resonance and total irresistibility …

Dedication

Dedication

As always, I prevailed upon Martin Dobbs to critique various drafts of the manuscript. Happily, he complied and this, along with all the Romancing books is infinitely better as a result. I'm forever grateful and cannot imagine publishing a book without you. On the wider business front you are insightful, thought-provoking, encouraging and unfailingly wise, and when I think about what you have done for me I feel as lucky as any person alive.

I owe thanks to my parents, Brian and Jenny, who instilled such worthy values, and taught me many lessons about compassion, kindness, humility and the meaning of work. For your belief, understanding, humour and unconditional love – thank you x. What more could a child ask from their parents?

Two people finally have my deepest gratitude – Liz and Tony Perkins who have seen me through the toughest times, the massive disappointments, the shattered hopes, and the broken dreams. Sharing with me and understanding the risks involved and the sacrifice made. Ultimately for investing in an idea yet unproven … oh, yeh, and for copious amounts of rich red wine – hic!

THE BARRY WHITE EFFECT – yeh baby!

Contents

	Introduction	13
CHAPTER ONE:	Do you want my *!?@! money or not?	19
CHAPTER TWO:	All went well 'til the words came out!	23
CHAPTER THREE:	Speaking the right language	35
CHAPTER FOUR:	The four most useless words in retail	43
CHAPTER FIVE:	Every encounter counts	51
CHAPTER SIX:	The Bananarama moment	63
CHAPTER SEVEN:	Voices in my head	73
CHAPTER EIGHT:	Why don't these idiots get it?!!?	81
CHAPTER NINE:	Conclusion	85
	About the author	89
	What people say about Angi Egan	93

Introduction

Introduction

The Barry White Effect – yeh baby! is the third in the series of Romancing the Customer™ business guides; an impish and fresh insight into the principles of creating powerful brand differential and longevity. It runs the parallel between great romance and great business and how, by stimulating all of the senses and focusing on creating lasting relationships, both business and consumer can enjoy memorable experiences.

This book focuses on the auditory aspect of your business – anything from voicemail to inner dialogue, from natural conversations with our customers to inspiring communication with the people who work with us. Its aim is to share some of the ways in which you can create powerful connections, or where you may be 'destroying the moment' purely through the words you use. This is more than simply a thoughtless word or a clumsy mumble – how we communicate has become central to how, as business leaders, we inspire, educate and create a brand that great people aspire to work for and consumers find completely irresistible.

THE BARRY WHITE EFFECT – yeh baby!

Communication is the key to brand success and our capacity to embrace the potency of words will enrich the lives of both businesses and their customers. These principles have stood the test of time and are so obvious they often get overlooked, or worse still, they're mistaken as soft, fluffy skills that have no credible place in modern commerce.

Romancing the Customer™ is a straightforward message about the strength of relationships and a strong brand message. This is what will separate the good from the exceptional during the next decade, and will also be the barometer for consumers about where they choose to place their loyalties, and ultimately their diminishing spend.

There are many comparisons between strong business relationships and captivating romance. It all begins with the eye-catching, foot-faltering, head-turning mm mmm of Initial Lust, the first book in the series; it is intensified by arousing the other four senses, and is prolonged through a masterful attention to create everlasting longing.

Espresso Yourself was the second in the series and involved the taste, or perception of your brand. It discussed the need to 'interrupt the pattern' of our

INTRODUCTION

customers by surprising and delighting them during every encounter. To wake them from their weary tedium by introducing a determined strategy which sweeps away the dull and predictable. To create that much-needed differential. A differential that is exclusive to you and your organisation, is totally authentic and therefore less likely to be copied. A differential which lasts.

Ideas presented throughout *The Barry White Effect – yeh baby!* are in many ways the simplest to introduce to your business and everyday thinking. Simple, not easy.

Although challenging they bring rich rewards. As with our personal relationships, the ability to communicate with humour, integrity and consideration will ensure we create lasting memories and unbridled passion in the hearts and minds of our customers – for us, for our products, for our services.

It requires discipline and awareness. It requires an investment in time. It involves not only the power of language – internal and external – it also considers the impact of a rapidly diminishing skill … the power of listening.

In a world where the drive to better, bigger and best appears to surpass any other consideration we are in danger of obscuring the simple steps needed

THE BARRY WHITE EFFECT – yeh baby!

to create successful businesses. Success that is measured not just by profits. It must now include the relevance and significance a business has in both the consumer's and employee's life. And this begins with asking, listening and behaving with transparency and integrity. Understanding problems is no longer enough. We must now demonstrate we understand the issues caused. Only then can we add value.

Many British businesses see this as somehow acting in a submissive manner, of being a wimp, or being a pushover and so overcompensate by refusing to listen to their employees and customers or ever considering that maybe, just maybe, their approach may be wrong. Should they decide to continue with this attitude these businesses will discover they are terribly mistaken.

Throughout the book we will look at ways in which you may be unwittingly undermining your authority and by doing so, the confidence of your team and your customers. I have always believed that few people deliberately set out to sabotage their own success (*and where it happens is a whole other book!*) they do so through being unaware.

Through the principles of Romancing the Customer™ I hope to raise this awareness with simplicity, humour and good old common sense.

CHAPTER ONE

......

"Do you want my *!?@! money or not?"

"Do you want my *!?@! money or not?"

This was suggested as the title of one of my books so I thought it would make a wonderfully potent beginning to *The Barry White Effect* – yeh baby!

Heartened that I'm not alone in despairing of service on our high streets I also find myself slightly depressed by the lack of impetus by businesses to 'get it'. Brands continue to pour huge sums of money into all-singing, all-dancing adverts which promise such wonderful things. Then we visit the store and feel let down by breathtakingly bad service.

When will brands, retailers in particular, start to understand that the most pure form of brand experience is the encounter we have in their stores, not the glossy communication which tempted us there in the first place? In many ways this inconsistency of the brand 'experience' does lasting damage beyond anything else they might conceive of. The communication instore, or lack of, is something that continues to drive consumers bonkers!

I know I'm not alone in longing to be served by individuals who are interested, enthusiastic, polite

THE BARRY WHITE EFFECT – yeh baby!

and committed to serve. As I approach an age which qualifies me for 'grumpy old woman' status I have become so irritated by the lacklustre, indifferent service from individuals who don't have a clue about the products they're selling. By business leaders who talk a good media talk but offer a 'one-size-fits-all' training programme because they have no idea how to make the generational leap in communication needed to engage and inspire their young workforce. By brands who believe we're so dumb we won't spot their cynical and contrived marketing.

Think for a moment about an electrical retailer who repositioned themselves from price driven to service focused midway through 2009. The only flaw? They forgot to communicate this to the individuals responsible for delivering the service! Their stores continue to ignore customers, fail to know anything about the white goods they assert to be experts in, and finally insist on selling us extended warranties we don't want or need. In fact, the very brand who inspired the title of this chapter. Sadly there are countless others who fall into the category of "Hello?? I'd like to buy something, please".

Communication, both with the teams employed and the consumers we're aiming to attract, will be the key to business success as we speed headlong into the twenty-first century. Without humility, arrogance and conceit become inevitable bedfellows.

"DO YOU WANT MY *!?@! MONEY OR NOT?"

The key to successful communication in both business and leadership is that paradoxical combination of skills – humility and fierce resolve.

Humility to serve with pride. Fierce resolve to ensure every communication supports this ambition. Until businesses understand the principle of serving the consumer instead of serving their own operational and corporate needs then we will continue to question our loyalty to them. They will always struggle to retain great staff. They will always blame suppliers. They will always find excuses. They will always find reasons why it's not their fault. And they will always be searching for that elusive loyal customer.

The common denominator is not transient staff, poor suppliers, market conditions, banks, government, global influences, the internet or promiscuous consumer behaviour – it rests firmly at the feet of the brand leaders to communicate authentically, honestly and free from any hint of BS. The alternative simply creates cynicism, indifference and mistrust.

Let's begin by looking at the different areas of our verbal communication and see where this might just be creating the doubt, boredom and lack of confidence I'm describing. I touched on this in *Espresso Yourself* as an easy way to create brand differential by daring to be just a little bit different.

• • •

CHAPTER TWO

......

All went well 'til the words came out!

All went well 'til the words came out.

One of the simplest steps anyone or any business can take is to create an inspiring and refreshingly different voicemail. Done badly, and faster than you can imagine, it becomes an area that will undermine both the professionalism and the quality perception of your brand. Done well and it will impact on how much I'm prepared to pay for your services and products, how quickly I'm prepared to trust you and even whether I'm even prepared to do business with you.

Voicemail is simple to change and can do more to build anticipation, create interest and communicate how you do what you do than any other area in *The Barry White Effect – yeh baby!* arena – and it costs nothing. Free. Nada. Nowt. Gratis.

I have mentioned the need to interrupt the pattern of anticipated behaviour in *Initial Lust* and *Espresso Yourself*. This not only helps to create differential in the mind of your customer it also helps to create a talking point, it wakes them up a little, gives you an opportunity to describe what you can do for me, and finally, lightens up an otherwise predictable day.

THE BARRY WHITE EFFECT – yeh baby!

It is also essential when communicating with potential and existing customers why you're 'the one'.

Most businesses will have something along the lines of "Thank you very much for calling, sorry I'm not free to take your call … blah blah blah". Brain-numbingly boring and generic. A voicemail that sounds just like every other organisation you encounter in fact. Anything from government agencies to the local plumber. This is a great strategy to employ if you're happy to be part of a colossal herd of faceless, unimaginative businesses yet of little help if your intention was to stand out from the crowd, create allure and pique curiosity.

> *"In order to be irreplaceable one must always be different"*
> Coco Chanel

It is worth taking the time to craft a voicemail that communicates what you do – this includes mobiles as well as office phones. On the subject of mobiles, if you still have the generic phone provider message, then shame on you! It does nothing to establish you as an inspired, committed professional; in fact, it suggests you either can't be bothered or you're completely unaware – neither of which is an attractive quality.

This is the first example of something being simple, not easy. If it were easy everyone would do it – creating powerful messages takes time but it is worth it. This step in your communication strategy guarantees you stand out from the crowd.

Mobile phones

Commit now to stop promoting your mobile phone provider; instead use your voicemail message to promote you and your business. Change this and I promise it will create a response – if only to confirm customers have reached the right person!

The following are some tips to crafting a memorable voicemail that gets customers talking – and hopefully means they leave you a message.

- Take time to consider what it is you *do* – not what you *are* – accountants might help business owners relax because financial compliance is taken care of, hairdressers create wonderful styles, beauty therapists help make you look and feel gorgeous, dentists make smiles brighter, plumbers save a precious resource,

THE BARRY WHITE EFFECT – yeh baby!

photographers capture the moment, business coaches provide the vehicle to get you from A to B, dry cleaners keep you looking pressed and pristine … hopefully you're getting the idea.

- Script what you're going to say – you will sound much more professional. Practise reading this out loud several times before recording so you'll understand where to place emphasis and passion. This stops it sounding monotone and dull.

- Stop apologising! The Brits suck at service but we're world leaders at the apology. Start to think about what you're communicating – sorry for being successful/in demand/blooming marvellous? – I don't think so. Say sorry if you insist, just be aware of how distinctly average it makes you sound.

- Make the recording in a quiet place – ideally surround your phone with cushions to absorb those horrid tinny sounds and give a much-needed base tone to the recording.

- Avoid recording your message in the car, while walking, in a busy railway station, in the toilet, with the radio on or with your child/dog/hamster creating chaos in the background – I've heard them all and it doesn't sound good.

- Keep it short and sweet – avoid getting carried away and leaving a message so long callers lose the will to live before it ends, about 30 seconds, tops.

- Change it on a regular basis – about every 4–6 weeks should be enough depending on how regularly clients call you.

Here's an example of one I've used with great success –

"You've reached the voicemail for Angi Egan – I'm currently working with an exceptional business to help them identify where they can create bliss for their customers. If you're intrigued and would like to know more please leave your details and together we can discover what makes your business exceptional. Thank you and keep shining."

… takes about 15 seconds, is totally authentic, describes what I'm doing, is miles away from predictable and means callers leave a message (sometimes just to say they think I'm crazy, sometimes it's my mum calling to tell me if I'm with a client at 10pm on a Friday evening then she's appalled) whatever, my message interrupts the pattern and always creates a response.

THE BARRY WHITE EFFECT – yeh baby!

Office voicemail

- Same rules on scripting and recording in a quiet environment.

- If you have a menu option on your phone then please explain why you use it … If it really does get the best possible services for the caller describe how this is of help to me. Think about the caller – personally, automated menus frustrate the life out of me and are a perfect example of corporate thinking, not customer thinking "Press 1, press 2, press 3 … press 9 …" Arrrgh! For the love of God, I just want to speak to a human being!!! And I bet the majority of customers feel just the same.

- Be aware of the music on hold – a totally subjective area, I appreciate – but the music needs to reflect the personality of your brand and the profile of the majority of your callers. Few things are guaranteed to get callers madder than inappropriate music choices. If they hadn't phoned to complain they sure will after being subjected to loud, annoying sound tracks. Finally, adjust the volume – most music on hold blasts your head off.

ALL WENT WELL 'TIL THE WORDS CAME OUT!

- Tell me how long it is likely to be before you can call me back. A generic "I'm either away from my desk or on another call" says absolutely nothing and is stating the obvious. Rarely do I feel compelled to leave a message.

- Monitor how many people hang up and don't leave a message – this could be an area where you're forcing that much-coveted customer into the arms of your competition simply because the majority of people detest pesky voicemail systems.

If your aim is to enchant, seduce, charm and generally create an impact with customers then never assume your voicemail doesn't matter – it does. What you say on your voicemail will also create an expectation – please let it not be that you're predictable, dreary or unaware about how to captivate and inspire me.

> *"Your spark can become a flame and change everything"*
> ED Nixon

THE BARRY WHITE EFFECT – yeh baby!

Finally ask, ask and ask some more. Find trusted customers to give you honest feedback. Or give them a way of responding anonymously. At the very least call in to your own message occasionally and listen for yourself. I know a business whose particularly disgruntled receptionist changed the on-hold message the day she left. It took several months before a customer eventually asked the Managing Director if he was aware that every caller was listening to a message detailing how badly the company treated their staff, how unreasonable they were and how poor the quality of their services and products were. The ultimate revenge for sure, but illuminating nevertheless. How many people had listened to this, probably had a titter, but said nothing?

General recordings

Let me begin with a story of what I mean. There was a fabulous spa in Staffordshire, set in a truly unique and tranquil location, steeped in history and a total joy to read about in the brochure. Suitably enchanted I booked my treatments through their fantastic website and could hardly wait for the day to arrive. The brochure detailed how all treatments would begin with a relaxation exercise, perfect for individuals who fly around like a paper bag. This was described as a 'guided meditation' so I had anticipated a commentary of some sort. What I had not anticipated was the broad Hull accent which would accompany the commentary. It was such a distraction and eventually had me (and every other spa guest) giggling uncontrollably. Everything about the client journey had been so perfect, so luxurious, so totally five star that a strong accent of any kind just didn't fit. I simply couldn't understand how the owners could have misjudged this part of the client journey so badly.

I'm compelled to state at this point I have no issue with accents – my mum's broad Geordie, my dad's a Yorkshire man, I work in Birmingham for goodness sake! Simply be aware of how distracting strong accents are in a corporate recording. This doesn't mean speaking like you've got a plum in your mouth, using vocabulary that simply isn't you or anything which creates misleading glossiness. It means being aware of the distraction strong dialects create. In a corporate recording it just gets in the way of people listening to what is being said, whether we like it or not. Find the person who speaks the clearest or invest in a professional voice recording, it is necessary and will be worth it.

• • •

THE BARRY WHITE EFFECT – yeh baby!

I'm conscious that perhaps I have a higher awareness than most of the power of the voice to get a message across.

Firstly, I'm a professional speaker so have huge appreciation for people with the ability to charm and amuse through their words, their stories and their voice. Secondly, my only method of home entertainment is the radio. I mention this to describe how I find one well-known business commentator so irritating I can barely stop myself from throwing things at the radio when he comes on. He has the most infuriating way of talking! He places emphasis in all the wrong places, hesitates unnecessarily, appears to have no concept of voice modulation, and generally drives me to distraction. I could read his column all day long but when I hear him being introduced on the radio I would happily have him shot.

Rant over. Be aware of how powerful voice tone is to create an immediate connection with people – or not. I don't listen to a word he's saying because of the way he talks. I'm totally distracted. Get into the habit of asking customers how things sound rather than assuming it doesn't matter. It does and it will. Avoid the BTN syndrome (better than nothing) because BTN never is …

CHAPTER THREE

......

Speaking the right language

Speaking the right language

In social surroundings most of us moderate our language to reflect the environment. However, this is not what I'm talking about when I say speak the right language. I'm making reference to the way the words we use create that most coveted connection with people. And in a business environment, where we're looking to introduce what we can do for them, speaking the other person's language is essential. The common mistake is to start describing (selling) what you do before first establishing any kind of credibility in their mind. Wading in too fast with 'all about you' is just so inappropriate and can alienate you faster than a bad case of halitosis. Think carefully about the questions you ask and the things you're about to say to ensure you're not offending people.

If we run the parallel with dating it's the same as meeting someone for the first time and they begin to ask highly personal questions, or worse still, start to make inappropriate disclosures about themselves. It's simply too forward and leaves me feeling deeply uncomfortable, or massively hacked off! And so it is with business, telling me about your fantastic gizmo/service/opportunity before I've even said I'm looking for one is guaranteed to have me running for the nearest exit. Too many people focus on the services or products they want to sell or can provide, without asking and listening first. In fact, it seems to me the only reason they're listening in the first place is to justify what they were going to recommend.

> *"There are people who, instead of listening to what is being said to them, are already listening to what they are going to say themselves"*
> Albert Guinon

I made reference in *Espresso Yourself* about the need to craft a top five to understand about the hopes, dreams and desires of your prospective customer, to establish if they would even be interested in what you had to say, and to see if they were 'eligible' – do they have the budget for what you offer, for example? Speaking the right language goes one step beyond this.

SPEAKING THE RIGHT LANGUAGE

Today, more than ever, we have generations speaking what appears to be a completely different language, peppered with words that mean totally different things depending on what age we are. This isn't new; it is simply more acute than it once was. In a retail store I visited recently, for example, I was appalled to be met with "Awright mate, see anything you like?" This was from a young male that I'd never met before. I wasn't his mate. I was a customer looking to spend upwards of £2,000 on electrical goods. Suffice to say I didn't see anything I liked.

Or the young woman in a fashion retailer who as her opening gambit asked me "What exactly brought you into the store today?" … "Erm, my feet?" was what I was tempted to reply. Totally pointless questions as far as I was concerned, although I suspect totally legitimate from their perspective.

Speaking the right language means understanding the values of the person you're talking to – as far as possible. This requires more questions, more listening and more understanding than ever before. It's the old maxim – you can have the best product in the world but if you're talking in a way that alienates me or majors on solutions I'm not looking for, then I'm never going to buy it from you. There are countless

THE BARRY WHITE EFFECT – yeh baby!

tomes dedicated to 'closing' the sale but the truth is if they don't want something you can 'close' until you're blue in the face, they'll never take it.

For example, selling skincare or cosmetics to one of my sisters is a walk in the park – providing you tell her it's used by the latest celeb and will make her look younger, she'll part with huge sums of cash. Talk to her about ingredients, environmental credentials or how natural it is and she's likely to keel over from boredom.

With techie stuff, talk to me about gigabytes/megabytes/love bites et al and my eyes are likely to glaze over. Fail to mention this to my best friend and you'll lose the sale.

It can be a minefield – but it doesn't need to be. Observing some basic rules of natural conversation and asking the right questions can quickly establish the right tone and language to use in order to create a great impact.

Conversations need to be relaxed. It's not always *what* you ask or say, it's *when* you ask or say it. Keep your conversations, well … conversational! Avoid letting your eagerness to make a great impression or introduce your products overwhelm

SPEAKING THE RIGHT LANGUAGE

people, I see and experience this so many times – and find it so off-putting. Simply have a conversation and share what you have when it's appropriate.

This is what I have described as the flirting and showing off stage. Flirting is about finding something lovely to say about the other person simply because you can. It has no agenda other than to create a connection. It could be a comment about an unusual piece of jewellery, or a striking outfit, smart business card, interesting point they've just made – anything in fact. A word of caution, however – keep this non-personal. Commenting on hair/fragrance/eyes/height/body parts *et al* often makes people feel incredibly self-conscious and uncomfortable in your company if you're in a formal business meeting. Respecting personal boundaries is vital when aiming to create a connection. An obvious point you might be thinking, yet I'm amazed how many times this happens.

Consider how you respond to compliments – Brits have a wonderful way of throwing them back at people by saying things like "What – this old thing?" or "Really? I'm a bit bored with it" or anything else which effectively rejects the opinion of the person making the comment. How about being refreshingly different and simply saying a

THE BARRY WHITE EFFECT – yeh baby!

gracious thank you? Relaxed conversations need to be genuine; this will then allow you to bring what you do into the conversation when it feels natural and right to do so. This is what I mean when I say showing off. It is simply listening out for the need/interest/want to know more about element of the conversation. When you show off it is simply to demonstrate how you've helped others with the same thing in the past by perhaps saying something like "Oh, that's interesting. One of my clients described something similar and we were able to work together to solve it by ..."

Showing off is a wonderful way of establishing credibility in the mind of the other person without ever falling into the fatal trap of being the big 'I am'. Showing off at the appropriate moment will do more to communicate your knowledge, endorse your reputation and highlight your credentials than any other business strategy you might employ. I use it all the time: sometimes it generates business, sometimes it doesn't. Either way I know I will have shared something of value with the other person without ever compromising my brand integrity or reputation. I'm a great advocate of 'show me, don't tell me' and the showing off approach allows you to demonstrate your knowledge far more effectively than simply telling people how much stuff you know.

"People don't care how much you know until they know how much you care"

Theodore Roosevelt

Above all else practise, practise, practise. Practise with real people all the time. Practise one thing at a time in small steps. Notice how people's attitudes toward you change as you progress. You can't learn to swim from a book, at least I don't think you can, and natural conversations are no different – you need to try it out and see what works for you. Significance, relevance and heightened awareness will follow as you get more familiar with the process. The objective is not about making things perfect, it's about making the connection.

CHAPTER FOUR

······

The four most useless words in retail

The four most useless words in retail

Despite having spent many years working in retail I cannot bear 'shopping'. I take an SAS approach with my own retail habits – get in, get what I want, get out. I do, however, love creating the theatre and implicit thrill of great retail – I could study people's buying behaviour for hours (perhaps I should get out more) and few things offer me more pleasure than knowing I have used subtle skills to seduce someone into indulging in a little, but highly pleasurable, retail therapy. And although increasingly rare, I also love it when it happens to me. What can be better than to be charmed for a few moments by an enlightened, knowledgeable and enthusiastic retailer?

OK, it may not rate highly on your list of favourite indulgences but consider the last time an encounter in a retail situation made you smile, created great anticipation, left you longing to get home to open your purchase, or simply inspired you with a little knowledge.

Like I said, increasingly rare but not yet totally extinct. What will put this on the endangered species list is the one-size-fits-all approach being implemented up and down our high streets by our beloved but play-it-safe retailers. These are the ones whose retail director will have returned from a trip to America or SE Asia where they have been blown away with the service and attention to detail. They then attempt to apply the principles here and fall short because they fail to grasp the concept of individual empowerment (I bet that sentence on its own is the thing of nightmares to these people – tee hee jinksie).

Natural conversations in retail can never be prescriptive. They don't follow a script. They have no agenda. And they never start with the dreary and most useless words in retail: "Can I help you?" I believe anyone using this as their opening line deserves at the very least, a resounding thump (harsh but effective, of course, I mean this metaphorically).

Of course we're going to respond to "Hello, can I help you?" with "No, just looking, thanks" even when we're not, it's habit, it's a pattern. So, for the retail directors who may have nightmares, here are a couple of opening lines that may just inspire, connect and bliss your customers out.

It starts by watching what the customer is looking at and commenting on the product and inviting some reaction/feedback/remark … before you know it a natural conversation begins.

THE FOUR MOST USELESS WORDS IN RETAIL

"That's a great fragrance isn't it?"

"That's our most popular …"

"Customers have been raving about that …"

"Great choice. That colour looks perfect on you/really suits you."

"There's so much choice here, isn't there – can I help you find anything?"

"I'm thinking of buying one of these. They're fabulous for …"

"This one is my favourite too."

"That's just arrived."

If the customer is about the same age as your mum/dad/nephew/best friend then you could consider starting the conversation with "My niece thinks that's the best thing since …"

This can sometimes go a little awry, but hey, that's part of the fun isn't it? I recall saying to a guy who was buying the latest movie starring Jennifer Aniston, how gorgeous she was in it. Offering me the most withering look he replied, "I'm buying it to watch Vince Vaughn actually." Oops! See what I mean.

Once the conversation has progressed and you have a little more understanding then use gentle statements such as:

"You might like to consider …"

"Have you thought about …?"

"Perhaps you'd like to try …?"

"Many people aren't aware that …"

And if things are really going to plan and you've made a wonderful connection you could dare to be different by making a more enthusiastic recommendation:

"I think you're going to prefer …"

"This goes brilliantly with what you've chosen. What do you think?"

"If you love that then you'll probably love this too."

THE FOUR MOST USELESS WORDS IN RETAIL

"That colour looks great, can I suggest this one as an alternative? I think it'll really enhance your features."

"I'll tell you what goes well with this …"

This is far more enthusiastic and compelling than the generic, monotone attempts at link sales seen in some of our banks and retail stores at the till point. "Do you want a bag of half price Haribo jelly bears?" … Do I look like I eat Haribo jelly bears?

Or how about in banks – "It says on the screen you're self-employed. Have we spoken to you about business banking, Miss Egan?" Erm, yes – in fact every time I come into the bank.

Worse still is when they ask, "Can I do anything else for you today?" In a moment of deep mischievousness I once replied, "Oh yes, if you don't mind, could you collect my dry cleaning, walk the dog and do my grocery shop while I have my hair cut please?" I swear the cashier checked her script for 'likely replies' before she said, "Sorry, I don't finish work until 5pm and I don't think we're allowed to do any of that." Oh dear.

THE BARRY WHITE EFFECT – yeh baby!

I appreciate they're only trying to be nice, and it's a heap better than being totally ignored, however, these generic responses lack any personality or sincerity which inevitably leads to cynicism (or in my case being a smartalec!).

Ultimately we all love it when we're in the hands of a confident, enthusiastic and interested person, and in business and retail it seems this skill is being compromised for the sake of playing safe with generic and homogenised dialogues.

Two of the best for effortless and consistently uplifting service would for me be Apple stores and Jo Malone. Visit them just for the experience and you'll see some of the best flirting and showing off there is in retail. Just remember to take your credit card – you'll be driven mad with desire otherwise!

CHAPTER FIVE

......

Every encounter counts

Every encounter counts

I'm a pretty confident kind of girl, can small talk with the best of them and reckon I can strike up a conversation with most people, so walking into a room full of strangers rarely fazes me. I also tend to stand about a foot above most people so surveying the area once I'm in there is no problem either. However, I have grown to loathe business networking events. It appears to be the realm of the perpetually tedious or the overenthusiastic.

Perpetually tedious because for some people they appear to be there for no other reason than to save them having to think about what to have for breakfast/lunch/dinner. They ask the same question of every person, the answer to which they're not listening to, then prattle on about where their office is, how long they've been doing what they do, how many people they employ and how busy sick they are (definition of busy sick – when people groan "Oh, I'm just *soooo* busy") which always leaves me wondering, how come you're sitting here then? Once I have removed my fork from their eye I generally encounter the 'overenthusiastic' networker.

THE BARRY WHITE EFFECT – yeh baby!

These can be easily recognised by the fact that they shake your hand and simultaneously slap your back if you're a guy, or insist on kissing you if you're a woman. Yuk. They ask for your business card in the first ten seconds (refuse to give it to them, it's ever so funny) while telling you all about them, ending with "I think we should meet up for coffee" (a euphemism for "I'd like a couple of hours free consultancy"). They also make the assumption that you'll happily introduce them to your clients and give them loads of business.

So, in order to avoid the pitfalls of a fork in the eye consider the following to create memorable connections:

If the four most useless words in retail are "Can I help you?" then the equivalent at a networking event must be "What do you do?" (*think – "Hello darling, do you come here often?" It really is that naff.*)

The first objective must be to establish common ground. You are, or at least ought to be, focused on discovering how interesting this person is before deciding to share your stuff. This is the 'be selective not desperate' element explained in *Espresso Yourself* – wading in with 'all about you' sends out a totally negative message and suggests you're prepared to do business with almost anyone.

EVERY ENCOUNTER COUNTS

Great networking is about discovering what it is about this person that makes them interesting rather than what it is they do. Building rapport and creating connections could start in any of the following ways:

"How did you find out about this event?"

"Who do you know here?"

"What do you think makes this club/event successful?"

"So, you attend a few different networking events. What is it you like best about networking?"

You could start natural conversations by commenting on topical and relevant events in the news or on TV (not a total killer for those without TV, as this by itself is a great conversation starter).

"What do you think about …?"

"Did you hear the report on the radio about …?"

"Interesting you mention that, there was a programme about that yesterday. Did you see it?"

"Did you read in the paper about …?"

THE BARRY WHITE EFFECT – yeh baby!

"Do you follow …?" Choose a programme (generally *X Factor* or *Strictly* although could be *Spring Watch*).

Each reply will offer you a more detailed picture about this person if you're really listening and is rather brilliant for establishing common ground.

You could always make a statement about their reply:

"That's interesting, I agree …"

"Oh, I believe…" and possibly take the opposite view (especially for 'talent' contestants).

A great way of finding out more information is to make the other person feel as comfortable as possible in your company. This way they're more inclined to share their thoughts and feelings without you firing 20 questions at them in the style of the Spanish Inquisition. Carefully listening to each reply and using these to demonstrate you've heard what they've said has to be the most sincere and highly complimentary way of showing people you're listening rather than waiting to speak.

I find these questions tend to get much more information, in a much faster way, and best of all

EVERY ENCOUNTER COUNTS

it means 'every encounter counts' – you will most definitely make a positive and glowing impression upon the other person:

"How do you mean?" (Avoid "What do you mean", which often sounds rude and aggressive.)

"What happened next?"

"Like what?"

"How does that work?"

"What else?"

Beginning with building rapport and creating connections is fabulous as this leads beautifully and elegantly into finding out what they do without ever asking the dreaded "What do you do?"

If you're wondering 'how' then consider the following alternatives:

"From what you've said about … it sounds like you're deeply interested in … is this the kind of business you have?"

"You sound very creative. This suggests you're a … "

THE BARRY WHITE EFFECT – yeh baby!

"You've said you love nature programmes and you've mentioned *Farming Today* – are you a vet by any chance?" (or anything around what they've been talking about).

And voila! You have made sure every encounter counts, you've discovered lots of things about the other person, you've established common ground, and you've avoided being predictable.

Next it's time to get them to ask the $6 million question: "What's that then?" (make a game of it and award yourself bonus points every time someone asks you this). Assuming most people will begin with the dreaded four words (because not everyone has been lucky enough to read this book) use the opportunity to surprise and delight them with your response by describing what you do for your customers rather than what you do for a living (perhaps go back to the chapter on voicemail messages if you haven't thought about this yet).

Using a little humour and a bit of gentle teasing would be effective at this point especially if you feel the other person isn't really listening. I've found one of two things happen by saying something different – you either fully capture their attention or they make a standard reply, confirming your sense that they're not

EVERY ENCOUNTER COUNTS

listening, at which point I make a swift exit – more on swift exits down the page …

Let's look at a few scenarios:

How not to do it –

"Hello, I'm Nigel and I am an undertaker, what do you do?"
"Hello, pleased to meet you. My name's Angi, I'm a business consultant."
"Oh right." (That went well then …)

And the alternative –

"Hello, I'm Nigel and I'm God's tour operator."
"Ha ha ha …what's that then?" … Bingo, you're off!

When faced with the four most useless words I might reply in any number of different ways –

"Hi, I'm Nigel. What do you do?"
"Hello, I'm Angi. I have a great job for a woman – I get paid to talk."
"Ha ha ha …what's that about then?"

Or   "I'm an author and I get paid for showing off on stage."

Generally followed by –

"I'm a professional speaker and I present at conferences my ideas for Romancing the Customer."
"Romancing the Customer sounds intriguing, what's that then?" (*Good at this game, aren't I?*)

Doing the network dance

From time to time we will encounter someone who doesn't 'float our boat', who we struggle to connect with, has an unfortunate case of halitosis, or who we simply find mind-numbingly dull. When this happens we still need to remain gracious, polite and professional while at the same time removing ourselves as fast as we can. This is where learning some moves from the network dance will become invaluable.

Take 'em and dump 'em

OK, so you find yourself in networking no-man's land and you need to get back to safe cover. Having been in this position many times, I find it helps to find a small group of people close by who you can subtly recommend joining. This simple dance move then allows you to make introductions while at the same time making a quick exit.

A lovely way of doing this is to say something like "Nigel has just been talking about his ideas for … which I thought you'd be interested in" or "This is Nigel and he's been sharing his thoughts on … I wondered what you make of them". No one is offended. You've behaved impeccably. Your reputation is intact. And you've just introduced them to people they may never have had the nerve to approach. More importantly, you're free to continue networking.

Of course there are thousands of excellent books on networking skills and strategies which can supplement this introduction to networking. The Romancing the Customer™ approach is about establishing common ground, discovering more about the other person, making the other person feel comfortable with you, creating powerful connections, building your reputation as a positive and glowing individual, and ultimately avoiding the 'what do you do' question!

Are you listening or waiting to make your point?

Listening to others is a rapidly diminishing quality; everyone seems to be on such a mission that they seldom hear what's being said. Yet when we truly receive the gift of being heard, or better still can offer this to someone else, the impact is very powerful.

Starting a conversation with a clear intent to listen creates a lasting and potent impression on the other person. Rarely do they know why (my guess? Because it's so unfamiliar!), they just feel great in your company, they can't wait to meet you again, and you become totally irresistible.

In a sales environment being able to truly listen is rare – mostly because we're either excited about communicating the possibilities we can offer, or because we're desperate for the sale. These are deeply unattractive characteristics and can often create the wrong impression on our potential customer.

Too many people focus on the services or products they want to sell or can provide without asking any questions beforehand. We must create that elusive credibility and trust before talking about ourselves as mentioned in Chapter 3: 'speaking the right language'.

Have you ever been in a position where you realise the only reason they have been allowing you to speak is to justify what they want to recommend? It's as though their only success is defined by getting customers to buy. For me it's like going to see your GP and they already know what prescription they're going to give you.

EVERY ENCOUNTER COUNTS

Here's a couple of ways to start to demonstrate your listening skills and at the same time create relevance and credibility:

"I have often found … I don't know if that's relevant, I wondered if you have ever experienced this type of situation?"

"I don't know if this would be valuable but … "

"I'd be interested to understand your feelings on … "

"Other customers have described … what are your thoughts?"

"I apologise if you already know this … "

This last one is wonderful simply because we often assume people understand the options and choices available so we fail to mention essential points for fear of stating the obvious or patronising customers. This question avoids either of these happening.

Sometimes because we're living with solutions everyday it starts to devalue what we know.

CHAPTER SIX

......

The Bananarama moment

The Bananarama moment

This has nothing to do with big hair, leggings, Siobhan or anything else associated with this 80s' pop group, it's just how my mind works. The Bananarama moment is all about the 'it ain't what you do it's the way that you do it' aspect of your business communication – presentations.

I know I'm not alone at feeling total despair when forced to listen to really poor speakers, Lord knows there are plenty of them out there.

I know from the coaching work I get involved with that most people's fear is that they don't have anything interesting to say. This is almost always unfounded and is the subject of the 'Voices in my head' chapter later on in the book.

Fear of speaking in public is something I battled with for years. I used to stand up to speak and my mind used to sit back down. Worse still was the time I was speaking at a huge international meeting as part of my job and halfway through my voice took on a life of its own, deciding it would be far more fun to make me warble like Katherine Hepburn in *On*

THE BARRY WHITE EFFECT – yeh baby!

Golden Pond – a deeply humiliating experience. I now speak for a living and love every minute.

Every single one of us is presenting ourselves in some way everyday. Be this in a formal way at a networking meeting, club, event, to our business associates, teams that work for us, or prospective customers, we will be required, at some point, to open our mouths to speak.

We owe it to the quality reputation of our brand to ensure what we say is always memorable, significant and the best we can possibly be.

There is an assumption that because you're the CEO or MD of an organisation (or a gifted accountant/dentist/manager/plumber/designer) you will automatically be an amazing presenter of your services or products. Or, as often happens, you start your own company and suddenly you're thrust into situations where you're speaking in public.

Some of the worst presentations I have ever had to endure were from individuals representing big-name brands. This suggests to me they've either never asked for feedback and assume they're fab, they're awful but no one ever tells them (or sadly employees lie and say they were great – they're the boss after all) or finally they know they're awful but imagine it doesn't matter. It most definitely does.

THE BANANARAMA MOMENT

Please take time to consider what it is you want to say and how you'd like to say it. Never ever, ever, ever start a presentation (even to your team) without preparation. It will be doing huge damage to you and your professional reputation. Like many of the elements of Romancing the Customer™ it really does communicate much more about your competency, how much I'm going to trust you, how much I'm prepared to pay for your goods and services – in fact everything about the quality of what you do.

If you have embraced the idea of 'every encounter counts' then this is never more relevant than when we are giving presentations. The best ones are made by those who understand the dynamic of creating lasting connections through talking with confidence, humour, authority and relevance – relevance to their audience and the things they would like to know more about.

Here are a few ideas to ensure you're presenting consistently well and to guarantee they create the impact you're aiming for – more business and an inspired team/customer.

Edit and revise the content

The common mistake when we're creating presentations is to say too much. Like visual pollution, people aren't able to understand our message when we're communicating too many things at once. I was taught early in my speaking career to see my presentations as diamonds – the more you cut them the more they sparkle.

Decide what message you absolutely must make to the audience and craft everything around this.

What are you aiming to influence?

What exactly do you want people to do as a result of listening to you? This should form the essence of your message. You need to be crystal clear and then apply the old adage – 'tell 'em, tell 'em, and tell 'em again' (not literally though, this would be really boring). Find different ways to communicate the same message. If you don't know what you expect people to do as a result of listening to you then your presentation becomes at best a pleasant way to pass half an hour, or a dreary waste of time at worst.

Why is this important?

A part of your Barry White Effect strategy is to understand that different people 'hear' things in different ways, and are therefore motivated to take action by different things. This is what I call the tears or tiaras aspect of communication.

Tears – Some people are hugely motivated by fear – of loss, of failure, of getting something wrong, doing a poor job, losing respect – often these guys will be inspired to act when you focus on the consequences of not acting on your message. For these people the avoidance of loss is a far greater motivator than the gain of reward.

Tiaras – Others are motivated by reward – bonuses, incentives, competitions, recognition, promotion, self respect, peer group approval, managers' appreciation – so these people will be ignited when you focus on the prize, reward or value to them aspect of your message.

To get consistently fab results with your presentations keep the focus of 'why is this important' on the audience rather than why it's important to you. Your audiences are seldom motivated by what's important to you. They will almost always be tuned into WIIFM (what's in it for me).

What makes you 'the one'?

This is the perfect opportunity to think about the ways you can show off and flirt. It may well be you're making the presentation because you're the boss or the company owner but this shouldn't stop you from charming and engaging with the audience. Remember – flirting is the saying something gorgeous, witty or

THE BARRY WHITE EFFECT – yeh baby!

gracious about them and showing off is demonstrating where this has been applied successfully before. Showing off with a team or a hesitant customer can mean the difference between them leaving loved up or leaving with a feeling of doubt and suspicion.

Showing off also makes it incredibly easy for people to raise concerns with you as it allows people to see how approachable you are, and at the same time reinforces your credibility in their mind. There is a train of thought which suggests avoiding raising concerns with customers at all costs. I think this is bonkers. I've always taken the view that concerns are buying signals so welcome and encourage them as much as possible.

Concerns are very different to objections – some may say this is female semantics – but what I've discovered is that objections are only ever made in response to my not fully understanding the customers' situation. This results in my making inappropriate suggestions or comments either because they have no relevance, or they're unsuitable, impractical or badly timed.

Be authentic

Stand tall and proud with your own achievements and never embellish to impress – it will come back to bite you! If you're presenting to your team then take 'ownership' of the message rather than blaming the board or the management for tough or difficult announcements. I always found myself doubting the confidence and leadership skills of someone who hid behind something or someone else instead of communicating with authenticity. Especially with unpleasant stuff – this is when you really do need to be authentic.

With an audience use your own material! Firstly few things are more boring than hearing a story you've heard before and when you know it belongs to someone else it can be infuriating … at the very least attribute stories and quotes to the originator.

Being authentic means no more than telling your own story and sharing your own experiences to the benefit of your audience.

Do your homework

Any presentation must be relevant to the audience so this means understanding what is of value to them, what will inspire, help, motivate, make life easier, and finally, what it is that they really want to know more about. If you don't do your homework it's like winking in the dark – in your world you're doing it but no one else can see it!

THE BARRY WHITE EFFECT – yeh baby!

What experience do you want to create?

Do you want to leave them feeling inspired, confident, amused, positive, convinced, intrigued, curious? Identify this and then craft how you're going to achieve it.

Finally seven top tips to focus your Barry White Effect thinking with presentations.

1. Be sure about what you're there for – understanding the purpose of why you? and why now? will make certain your presentation inspires, informs, influences and impresses.

2. Show passion! Heartfelt enthusiasm connects more powerfully than any other single thing. Yes, have a compelling message – just communicate it with passion.

3. Use stories to illustrate – you know the maxim 'stories sell, facts tell' – well, it's true. Use your own stories to give you confidence and provide that relaxed authority which means you create a powerful impact – every time!

4. Avoid lecturing – don't labour under the mistaken belief that what you say is the most important thing. It's not! Sure, content is important, but how you make

THE BANANARAMA MOMENT

people feel will have a far greater resonance. People often forget your words but they'll always remember how you made them feel.

5. Ditch the script – reading from a script fools no one – it just adds to the pressure you put yourself under. Perfection isn't connection and your aim must surely be to connect with the people you're talking to. Prepare your main points onto a prompt card and then speak from the heart, far more interesting and much more fun too.

6. Find different ways of communicating – always communicating in the same way suggests you don't care and lulls you to believe you're doing OK. If you haven't bothered to take the time to adapt what you're going to talk about to fit the needs of the listener, why on earth should they bother to pay attention to you? Understand who your audience is, what are their dreams, hopes, desires? What do they want you to solve for them? How can you do this better than anyone else? Why are you the answer to their dreams? Dare to be different – show off and flirt a little – it makes all the difference.

7. Move with purpose – never rock back and forwards, jangle things in your pocket, or worse still, put your hands in your pocket, wander about aimlessly or anything else that is massively distracting for the 'listener'. Standing still can add to your presence – providing you stand still with a purpose.

CHAPTER SEVEN

......

Voices in my head

Voices in my head

I know it's not just me who has a constant dialogue going on inside my head, or as my best friend Lizzie calls them, the Angi glove puppets. These are the kind of voices which tell you positive or negative things, either about yourself or about a given situation. Conquering or managing the glove puppets has, and continues to be, the biggest challenge I have, but a worthy discipline to introduce to my thinking.

I have finally accepted that the voices exist, I've even given the destructive one a name, so instead of providing her with any 'air time', I now acknowledge she's there and then tell her to sod off!

> *"Do not doubt yourself, for where doubt resides confidence cannot"*
> Jim Rohn

What my glove puppets have taught me is the value of words, and how, with just a few minor alterations

THE BARRY WHITE EFFECT – yeh baby!

we can significantly influence our emotions and subsequently our attitude. What we tell ourselves on a daily basis, or in the dead of night, soon becomes firmly planted into our consciousness which means it then soon becomes part of our attitude and behaviour. The great news is that we can change this thinking; it takes awareness and discipline, but it is worthwhile. Another example of simple, but not easy. Parallel to the glove puppets has been my learning from some fantastic and amazing people whom I have been fortunate enough to work with. Endlessly fascinated by what makes some people so compelling and what makes others, well, just plain dull, has occupied my thoughts for many years. Even before I knew what I was doing I believe I was observing how successful leaders managed to achieve such impressive results.

Equally I have also worked for, and with, some perfectly awful people, but hey, contrast is always necessary to achieve a full understanding! I did spend time thinking about what made some of my managers so bad, and it boiled down to their inability to communicate effectively. Sometimes they were horribly aggressive (which they dismissed as 'just being passionate') or they came across as monotone and weak. What it boils down to, apart from genuine passion and confidence, were the words they used on a regular basis.

VOICES IN MY HEAD

Rather typically for me I have created a top five of negative or vague words which I encourage you to banish from your vocabulary and replace with a more uplifting and distinct choice. If you're in a team or business environment play a game of buzz word bingo by making a list of the following words and see how many times they're used by those around you – hours of endless fun.

Try versus Aim – you've probably heard this before, especially if you're a *Star Wars* fan. Yoda was an instant hero of mine when he said, "There is no try, only do" – such a master of language. And yet he's got a point. How many times do you tell yourself or others you're going to try to do something? It just sounds so lame. You're either going to do something or you're not. It really is that straightforward. Alarm bells always sound for me when someone says, "I'll try to be there." What they really mean is, "I don't want to be there but I'm too polite to say no." Drives me insane.

'Hope' is another one and is very similar to 'try'. Consider how many times you use 'try' or 'hope' in your vocabulary, I promise you it sounds vague and lacking in any serious kind of commitment or authority.

THE BARRY WHITE EFFECT – yeh baby!

A replacement to 'hope' or 'try' is 'aim' – full of intention, meaning, resolve, purpose and far more inspiring and full of confidence.

Should versus Could – a real victim or judgement word, used when beating yourself up, or worse, someone else. You know the sort of thing: "I really should ... ", "You should ... ". People who regularly use 'should' are generally whining and moaning individuals whom I avoid as much as possible.

A more empowering word to replace should is 'could'. 'Could' suggests choice, which of course it is.

Why versus What – oh boy, this is such a good one. Having been the manager of some pretty large and diverse teams I learnt that not everyone does everything asked of them. Remarkable stuff, I know, and something I have struggled with (being a compliant and obliging type who does what I'm asked). I used to get pretty hacked off and wade in with "Why haven't you done ... ?" that is until I learnt the power of 'what' – "What has stopped you from ... ?" or "What would help you to ... ?" or the ultimate "What needs to happen for you to ... ?"

VOICES IN MY HEAD

It gets straight to the point because it doesn't put people on the defensive. Using the 'what' word seeks understanding without the other person feeling attacked. It also cuts through the waffle to communicate that you expect them to take responsibility and become accountable. And in a rather gorgeous way, if there has been a legitimate reason for something not being done it offers the other person a chance to explain without you looking like some aggressive and unreasonable so-and-so.

You could adopt this for home too – it's a marvellous way of avoiding scratchy rows while getting things done. Lovely.

Not versus Do – I don't know about you but I'm brilliant at knowing what I don't want and less brilliant at focusing on what it is I do want. Until that is, I discovered the power of 'dropping the not'. I was inspired by reading a chapter in one of John Humphrys' books where he described playing the game of not with the politicians and business leaders he interviewed. Apparently every time they preface any statement with 'not' he drops this and has hours of fun listening to them saying they "will put up taxes", they "will make budget cuts", they "have fudged their expenses" – whatever really, and it got me thinking. How many times do we say things like "don't look now" (and they look straight away), or "don't be late" (and they are) "don't forget" (and they do) "don't go mad" (and they do), "I don't mean to be rude" (mmm, yes you do).

And then there's not all by itself – I'm not judging (oh yes you are), I'm not blaming (got you again) whatever the circumstance 'I'm not' probably suggests you are. It is almost as bad as the 'but' word, almost but not quite. Simply put, hold in mind that almost everything that is said before a 'but' can be dismissed. It's a poor delaying tactic for when we have unpleasant and slightly controversial things to say.

Make versus Feel – I was taught to 'own the feeling' every time I said, "You make me … " mad, sad, angry, want to scream, happy, laugh – fill in as appropriate. This has proved to be so valuable when talking to co-workers, difficult customers or in personal relationships. I know I have driven friends bonkers in the past with "no one can make you feel anything" and it has cost me more than one relationship in the past because of their refusal to take ownership of what they were feeling. You will command far greater respect by taking control and personal responsibility for what and how you're feeling. The alternative is packed with blame and victim attitudes and is often horribly manipulative.

VOICES IN MY HEAD

So instead of "you make me" start to take control and replace this with "I feel".

I also discovered that our subconscious mind plays a similar sort of game with these negative words, although rather than for hours of amusement as in the case of John Humphrys, it's because our mind is like a Google search engine and is unable to process words of negation. Type in 'don't want chocolate' and see what happens. Lots of chocolate sites ping up!

So instead of starting our communication with 'don't' consider what it is we do want – "don't look now" becomes "when I tell you to, look behind you"; or "don't be late" becomes "please be on time", "don't forget" becomes "please remember", "don't go mad" is "please stay calm". In our conversations with family, friends, or employees dropping the 'don't' helps to focus the mind on what it is we're asking for in a clear and explicit way. Do this, I believe it is so powerful and stops all kinds of confusion and conflict.

CHAPTER EIGHT

......

Why don't these idiots get it?!!?

Why don't these idiots get it?!!?

Communication is the response we receive. Whoa, that's a profound statement to end the book with, yet true nevertheless. Getting people to understand what it is we're talking about and what it is we're aiming to communicate goes back to the Bananarama moment – it ain't what we say it's the way that we say it.

The golden rule with communication is one word: simplicity. In business using jargon is fatal, although I understand there is industry and profession 'speak' which becomes unavoidable, just be aware of how often you use this in your everyday language and especially with new employees or non-industry people. There was a time when I felt too afraid to say to one of my managers that I didn't have a clue what they were talking about so I just used to bluff and bumble my way through. Then I quickly realised that no one else really understood the gobbledegook this manager used so I decided to ask. Made life so much simpler!

THE BARRY WHITE EFFECT – yeh baby!

As with your advertisements and business cards (see *Initial Lust* for more details) say one thing that people can remember and take away with them. Simple messages reach the brain quicker and stay there for longer. Think what it is you need to say and then reduce it to as succinct a message as you can. You need to get people to engage with you as well as interrupting their thought process.

> *"Simplicity is the ultimate sophistication"*
> Leonardo da Vinci

Finally, if you want something done it's apparently a great idea to speak to a person's right ear. Scientists have discovered that because information received via the right ear is processed by the left-brain (logic, reason, fact) there is a greater willingness to carry out a request when delivered to that side (this is of course flawed in cases where the person is deaf in their right ear).

CHAPTER NINE

......

Conclusion

Conclusion

As with all of the Romancing the Customer™ business guides *The Barry White Effect – yeh baby!* is designed to challenge your thinking and offer suggestions about the simple ways you can create blissful moments for your customers – internal and external.

Internal customers are vital for how your brand is talked about, especially in the early days, anyone from the people you encounter at networking events, through to your suppliers, PA support, accountants as well as direct employees. Everyone needs to have the same ambition and understanding of your brand values.

Now more than ever we must create meaning and relevance in the minds of our customers and others we come into contact with. However fleeting, every encounter counts because you simply never know when you're creating a memory.

Communication is the lifeblood of any relationship and the quality of this communication is imperative to your and their lasting happiness. In business, as with our personal relationships, the ability to communicate with humour, integrity and consideration will ensure we create lasting memories and unbridled passion in the hearts and minds of those we're looking to romance.

Share my determination to replace the mundane with the inspirational, the predictable with the delightfully unexpected and the indifferent with the passionate. Invest in creating loyalty and understand this is never an overnight sensation – it requires discipline and consistency and above all – perseverance.

> *"You can't make footprints in the sands of time if you're sitting on your butt. And who wants to make buttprints in the sands of time?"*
> Bob Moawad

Become obsessive. Be fanatical. Add zest. Create bliss. Spread joy. Inspire. Educate. Get creative. Innovate.

Let's start a romance revolution …

About the author

About the author

Angi's retail pedigree is as diverse as it is distinguished – primarily with global household brands such as the Body Shop International, IKEA, Gap and M&S and finally with ESPA at Harvey Nichols and Liberty in London.

She has worked as a consultant with anything from cars, motorbikes, spectacles, skincare and wine merchants through to national charity organisations.

Within her retail career Angi gained knowledge and experience through successful senior management positions in all aspects that this multidiscipline profession demands – operations, marketing, shop floor, manufacturing and finally retail merchandising.

Developing and refining her understanding from some of the best retailers, Angi quickly established herself as a natural retailer who loved nothing better than the thrill of seeing customers buy. She also recognised her innate capacity to lead and inspire individuals to achieve team and personal goals.

THE BARRY WHITE EFFECT – yeh baby!

These are Angi's natural passions – retail and leadership – something she puts down to being 'proud to serve'. She discovered during her 20-year retail career that this requires dedication, courage, humility and commitment – some qualities she had in abundance, others she needed to discover through early mistakes.

With an instinctive feel for what works, what looks right and what will surprise and delight the customer, she is rapidly becoming recognised as one of the most innovative retail specialists.

Her approach is contemporary, highly relevant and totally fresh, and her overriding priority is to maintain a laser-like focus on the commercial gains open to the retailer.

Based in the historic jewellery quarter in Birmingham, she works with businesses across the UK and internationally.

What people say about Angi Egan

What people say about Angi Egan

"These great little books are perfect to get you thinking about how you look to your customers and how to improve your brand/image – I know Angi and it reflects her great insight and her humour – can't wait for the next one!"
Roni Flatley, Managing Director, Feel Good For Life

"Angi offers a refreshingly original view-point with an infectious enthusiasm about bringing passion to business. In today's environment of increasingly indistinguishable corporate promises, it is ever more important to distinguish ourselves from the competition. Angi's advice has been invaluable in helping us authentically express our genuine desire to help our customers."
Derek Watts, Managing Director, Nitritex Ltd

"I'm the first to admit that I'm a notoriously lazy reader. Angi Egan's light touch and conversational style is exactly what I hope for when I open a book. She is also refreshingly succinct – there's no jargon, no buzzwords – just clarity and common sense."
Rob Mainwaring, Operations Director, Whitehouse Mainwaring Design Consultants

"Should have a public warning attached – I laughed out loud with the cheeky style of writing but was impressed with the insights and approaches."
Bernard Molloy, CEO, HOPPECKE Industrial Batteries Ltd.

THE BARRY WHITE EFFECT – yeh baby!

"We will never do BTN again. Ever."
Karen Wharton, Director of Obsession Salon & Spas

"Being committed to my mission – Make Business Simple – Romancing the Customer™ does exactly that. The laws of romance can be understood by the majority and then simply translated into the seduction of clients. A perfect little book that can be read 'in an instance'."
Mike Pagan, Managing Director, Make Business Simple

"What I like most about this book is its simplicity in message yet maximum in effect!"
Peter Roper, Managing Director, Positive Ground

"A fun, refreshing and inspiring read, full of practicalities of how to approach retail differently in order to create lasting relationships and maximise sales."
Lindsay Webber, Client Services Director, Infinite Field Marketing Solutions

"Finally a narrative which cuts through generational gaps to communicate a traditional message in a way that means even the most cynical employee understands about service."
Jane Barnett, National Training Director, Kerastase Paris

"Angi has real warmth as well as creativity which makes everyone feel involved in reaching objectives."
Liz Holmes, Spa Director, Rockliffe Hall

Initial Lust: The Key To Visual Communication & Brand Marketing

The visual aspect of our brand is often the first thing which attracts attention – anything from our business cards and websites to how we present ourselves at meetings and events will be communicating the quality of what we deliver.

Too many times businesses are tempted to 'get stuff out there' in the mistaken believe that it's better than nothing (btn). Btn never is – everything about the visual communication of our brand must consistently reflect quality.

Initial Lust explores some of the ways you may be unwittingly sending out the wrong message – from business cards which suggest you're not going to be around very long to websites that 'we' all over their visitors or are plagued by visual clichés, this book will guide you through some of the common mistakes and offer examples on how to avoid it.

Initial Lust is the first step in creating a lasting brand differential and demonstrate how you're 'the one'.

Espresso Yourself: The Taste Of Your Brand

Taste, or the perception of your brand can be influenced by the little things which create a massive difference. This is one area that will do more to build trust, and so a loyal customer, than any other strategy you might be considering.

Exploring things such as employing people with a passion for your services through to providing inspired expertise to guarantee every customer leaves smarter than when they arrived will mean you start to move the focus from 'market share to mind share'.

Espresso Yourself provides a refreshingly different approach to creating brand fidelity and helping you avoid the curse of customer promiscuity.